This Journal Belongs to:

_____

_____

_____

*The LORD will keep you from all harm—
he will watch over your life; the LORD will watch over
your coming and going both now and forevermore.*

—PSALM 121:7–8

I guide you in the way of wisdom and lead you along straight paths.
When you walk, your steps will not be hampered;
when you run, you will not stumble.

—PROVERBS 4:11–12

Finally, brothers, whatever is true, whatever is noble, whatever is right,
whatever is pure, whatever is lovely, whatever is admirable—
if anything is excellent or praiseworthy—think about such things.

—PHILIPPIANS 4:8

The LORD watches over you—
the LORD is your shade at your right hand;
the sun will not harm you by day, nor the moon by night.

—PSALM 121:5

When you lie down, you will not be afraid;
when you lie down your sleep will be sweet.

—PROVERBS 3:24

*I delight greatly in the LORD;
my soul rejoices in my God. For he has clothed me
with garments of salvation and arrayed me in a robe of righteousness.*

—ISAIAH 61:10

_You have made known to me the path of life;
you will fill me with joy in your presence,
with eternal pleasures at your right hand._

PSALM 16:11

I love those who love me,
and those who seek me find me.

—PROVERBS 8:17

He will yet fill your mouth with laughter
and your lips with shouts of joy.

—JOB 8:21

Glory in his holy name;
let the hearts of those who seek the LORD rejoice.

PSALM 105:3

Humility and the fear of the LORD
bring wealth and honor and life.

—PROVERBS 22:4

*My soul glorifies the LORD
and my spirit rejoices in God my Savior.*

—LUKE 1:46–47

LORD, you have assigned me my portion and my cup;

you have made my lot secure.

—PSALM 16:5

For we are God's workmanship,
created in Christ Jesus to do good works,
which God prepared in advance for us to do.

—EPHESIANS 2:10

I praise you because I am fearfully and wonderfully made;
your works are wonderful, I know that full well.

—PSALM 139:14

He who fears the LORD has a secure fortress,
and for his children it will be a refuge.

—PROVERBS 14:26

I have loved you with an everlasting love;

I have drawn you with loving-kindness.

—JEREMIAH 31:3

For the LORD takes delight in his people;
he crowns the humble with salvation.

—PSALM 149:4

Many are the plans in a man's heart,
but it is the LORD's purpose that prevails.

—PROVERBS *19:21*

I tell you the truth, anyone who has faith in me will do what I have been doing. He will do even greater things than these, because I am going to the Father.

—JOHN 14:12

Guide me in your truth and teach me,
for you are God my Savior,
and my hope is in you all day long.

—Psalm 25:5

Trust in the LORD with all your heart and lean not
on your own understanding; in all your ways acknowledge him,
and he will make your paths straight.

—PROVERBS 3:5–6

He has made everything beautiful in its time.
He has also set eternity in the hearts of men;
yet they cannot fathom what God has done from beginning to end.

—ECCLESIASTES 3:11

*The LORD upholds all those who fall
and lifts up all who are bowed down.*

—PSALM 145:14

*The fruit of righteousness will be peace;
the effect of righteousness will be quietness and confidence forever.*

—ISAIAH 32:17

If you believe, you will receive whatever you ask for in prayer.

—MATTHEW 21:22

Commit to the LORD whatever you do,
and your plans will succeed.

—PROVERBS 16:3

I sought the LORD, and he answered me;
he delivered me from all my fears.

—PSALM 34:4

May God himself, the God of peace, sanctify you through and through. May your whole spirit, soul and body be kept blameless at the coming of our Lord Jesus Christ.

—1 THESSALONIANS 5:23–24

But God demonstrates his own love for us in this:
While we were still sinners, Christ died for us.

—ROMANS 5:8

He who conceals his sins does not prosper,
but whoever confesses and renounces them finds mercy.

—PROVERBS 28:13

But the eyes of the LORD are on those who fear him,
on those whose hope is in his unfailing love.

—PSALM 33:18

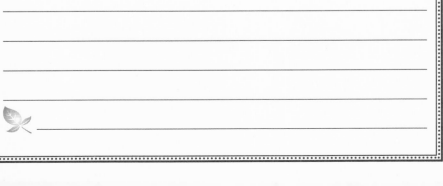

_____

_____

_____

_____

_____

_____

_____

_____

_____

_____

_____

_____

_____

_____

_____

_____

_____

_____

_____

_____

_____

_____

_____

_____

*Jesus replied, "If anyone loves me, he will obey my teaching.
My Father will love him, and we will come to him
and make our home with him."*

—JOHN 14:23

And we know that in all things
God works for the good of those who love him,
who have been called according to his purpose.

—ROMANS 8:28

For the LORD gives wisdom, and from his mouth come knowledge and understanding. He holds victory in store for the upright.

—PROVERBS 2:6

The LORD redeems his servants;
no one will be condemned who takes refuge in him.

—PSALM 34:22

For great is the LORD and most worthy of praise;
he is to be feared above all gods.

—1 CHRONICLES 16:25

"I will be a Father to you, and you will be my sons and daughters," says the Almighty.

—2 CORINTHIANS 6:18

The fear of the LORD is the beginning of wisdom,
and knowledge of the Holy One is understanding.

PROVERBS 9:10

Cast your cares on the LORD and he will sustain you;
he will never let the righteous fall.

—PSALM 55:22

Blessed are the pure in heart, for they shall see God.

—MATTHEW 5:8

We have this hope as an anchor for the soul, firm and secure.
It enters the inner sanctuary behind the curtain, where Jesus,
who went before us, has entered on our behalf.

—HEBREWS 6:19–20

_I_ will praise God's name in song and glorify him with thanksgiving.

—PSALM 69:30

So do not fear, for I am with you; do not be dismayed,
for I am your God. I will strengthen you and help you;
I will uphold you with my righteous right hand.

—ISAIAH 41:10

But godliness with contentment is great gain.

—I TIMOTHY 6:6

Let us not become weary in doing good,
for at the proper time we will reap a harvest if we do not give up.

—GALATIANS 6:9

And this is what he promised us—even eternal life.

—1 JOHN 2:25

As a father has compassion on his children,
so the Lord has compassion on those who fear him.

—PSALM 103:13

We wait in hope for the LORD;
he is our help and our shield. In him our hearts rejoice,
for we trust in his holy name.

—PSALM 33:20–21

Do not boast about tomorrow,
for you do not know what a day may bring forth.

—PROVERBS 27:1

Do you not know? Have you not heard?
The LORD is the everlasting God, the Creator of the ends of the earth.
He will not grow tired or weary, and his understanding no one can fathom.

—ISAIAH 40:28–29

Being confident of us, that he who began a good work in you will carry it on to completion until the day of Christ Jesus.

—PHILIPPIANS 1:6

May the LORD *direct your hearts*
into God's love and Christ's perseverance.

—2 THESSALONIANS 3:5

The LORD *is near to all who call on him,*

to all who call on him in truth.

—PSALM 145:18

The LORD *is full of compassion and mercy.*

—JAMES 5:11

*My son, keep your father's commands
and do not forsake your mother's teaching.*

—PROVERBS 6:20

_____

_____

_____

_____

_____

_____

_____

_____

_____

_____

_____

_____

_____

_____

_____

_____

_____

_____

_____

_____

_____

_____

_____

_____

"*For* I know the plans I have for you," declares the LORD,
"plans to prosper you and not to harm you,
plans to give you hope and a future."

—JEREMIAH 29:11

Be strong and take heart,
all you who hope in the LORD.

—PSALM 31:24

Every word of God is flawless;
he is a shield to those who take refuge in him.

—PROVERBS 30:5

Though the mountains be shaken and the hills be removed,
yet my unfailing love for you will not be shaken nor my covenant
of peace be removed," says the LORD, who has compassion on you.

—ISAIAH 54:10

*Your word is a lamp to my feet
and a light for my path.*

—PSALM 119:105

Therefore, since we are receiving a kingdom
that cannot be shaken, let us be thankful,
and so worship God acceptably with reverence and awe.

—HEBREWS *12:28*

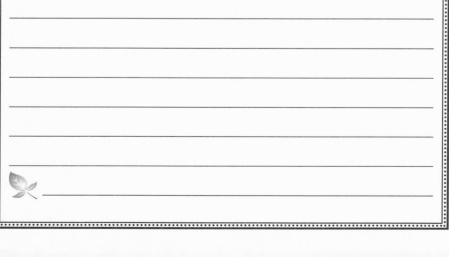

You are my lamp, O LORD;
the LORD turns my darkness into light.

He who dwells in the shelter of the Most High
will rest in the shadow of the Almighty. I will say of the LORD,
"He is my refuge and my fortress, my God, in whom I trust."

—PSALM 91:1–2

_____

_____

_____

_____

_____

_____

_____

_____

_____

_____

_____

_____

_____

_____

_____

_____

_____

_____

_____

_____

_____

_____

*A cheerful look brings joy to the heart,
and good news gives health to the bones.*

—PROVERBS 15:30

Give thanks to the LORD Almighty,
for the LORD is good; his love endures forever.

—JEREMIAH 3:11

*Lord, you have been our dwelling place throughout all generations.
Before the mountains were born or you brought forth the earth
and the world, from everlasting to everlasting you are God.*

—PSALM 90:1–2

Hope deferred makes the heart sick,
but a longing fulfilled is a tree of life.

PROVERBS 13:12

The Father himself loves you because you have loved me and have believed that I came from God.

—JOHN 16:27

My salvation and my honor depend on God;

he is my mighty rock, my refuge.

—PSALM 62:7

_____

_____

_____

_____

_____

_____

_____

_____

_____

_____

_____

_____

_____

_____

_____

_____

_____

_____

_____

_____

_____

_____

_____

A man's steps are directed by the LORD.
How then can anyone understand his own way?
—PROVERBS 20:24

Peace I leave with you; my peace I give you.

I do not give it to you as the world gives.

Do not let your hearts be troubled and do not be afraid.

—JOHN 14:27

I will lie down and sleep in peace, for you alone,

O LORD, make me dwell in safety.

—PSALM 4:8

Blessed is the man who finds wisdom,
the man who gains understanding, for he is more profitable
than silver and yields better returns than gold.

PROVERBS 3:13–14

_____

_____

_____

_____

_____

_____

_____

_____

_____

_____

_____

_____

_____

_____

_____

_____

_____

_____

_____

_____

_____

_____

_____

Be strong and courageous.
Do not be terrified; do not be discouraged,
for the LORD your God will be with you wherever you go.

JOSHUA 1:9

The wicked man flees though no one pursues,

but the righteous are as bold as a lion.

—PROVERBS 28:1

The LORD *is my light and my salvation—whom shall I fear?*
The LORD *is the stronghold of my life—of whom shall I be afraid?*

—PSALM 27:1

The LORD himself goes before you and will be with you;
he will never leave you nor forsake you.
Do not be afraid; do not be discouraged.

—DEUTERONOMY 31:8

God is our refuge and strength,
an ever-present help in trouble.

—PSALM 46:1

An anxious heart weighs a man down,
but a kind word cheers him up.

—PROVERBS 12:25

He is the Rock, his works are perfect, and all his ways are just.
A faithful God who does no wrong, upright and just is he.

—DEUTERONOMY 32:4

Be strong and take heart,
all you who hope in the LORD.

—PSALM 31:24

My son, pay attention to what I say; listen closely to my words.
Do not let them out of your sight, keep them within your heart;
for they are life to those who find them and health to a man's whole body.

—Proverbs 4:20–22

Do not grieve, for the joy of the LORD is your strength.

—*NEHEMIAH 8:10*

A heart at peace gives life to the body.

—PROVERBS 14:30

Though I walk in the midst of trouble, you preserve my life;
you stretch out your hand against the anger of my foes,
with your right hand you save me.

—PSALM 138:7

Draw near to God and he will draw near to you.

—JAMES 4:8

Praise be to the LORD, to God our Savior,

who daily bears our burdens.

—PSALM 68:19

In his heart a man plans his course,
but the LORD determines his steps.

—PROVERBS 16:9

The prayer of a righteous man is powerful and effective.

—JAMES 5:16

But as for me, I will always have hope;
I will praise you more and more. My mouth will tell of your righteousness,
of your salvation all day long, though I know not its measure.

—PSALM 71:14–15

A word aptly spoken
is like apples of gold in settings of silver.

—PROVERBS 25:11

_____

_____

_____

_____

_____

_____

_____

_____

_____

_____

_____

_____

_____

_____

_____

_____

_____

_____

_____

_____

_____

_____

_____

The LORD *gives strength to his people;*
the LORD *blesses his people with peace.*

—PSALM 29:11

The LORD will rescue me from every evil attack
and will bring me safely to his heavenly kingdom.
To him be glory for ever and ever.

—2 TIMOTHY 4:18

I have set the LORD always before me.
Because he is at my right hand, I will not be shaken.
Therefore my heart is glad and my tongue rejoices;
my body also will rest secure.

—PSALM 16:8–9

The name of the LORD is a strong tower;
the righteous run to it and are safe.

—PROVERBS 18:10

The LORD *will guide you always; he will satisfy your needs in a sun-scorched land and will strengthen your frame. You will be like a well-watered garden, like a spring whose waters never fail.*

—ISAIAH 58:11

Great peace have they who love your law,
and nothing can make them stumble.

—PSALM 119:165

The lamp of the LORD searches the spirit of a man;

it searches out his inmost being.

—PROVERBS 20:27

Surely the righteous will praise your name
and the upright will live before you.

—PSALM 140:13

_____

_____

_____

_____

_____

_____

_____

_____

_____

_____

_____

_____

_____

_____

_____

_____

_____

_____

_____

_____

_____

_____

_____

_____

_____

_I_ have given them the glory that you gave me,
that they may be one as we are one: I in them and you in me.

—JOHN 17:22

I have set the LORD always before me.

Because he is at my right hand, I will not be shaken.

—PSALM 16:8

For everyone born of God overcomes the world, even our faith.

—1 JOHN 5:4

Since you are my rock and fortress,
for the sake of your name lead and guide me.

—PSALM 31:3

_____

_____

_____

_____

_____

_____

_____

_____

_____

_____

_____

_____

_____

_____

_____

_____

_____

_____

_____

_____

_____

_____

This is love: not that we loved God,
but that he loved us and sent his son
as an atoning sacrifice for our sins.

—1 JOHN 4:10

Yet I am always with you;
you hold me by my right hand.

—PSALM 73:23

Do not wear yourself out to get rich; have the wisdom to show restraint.
Cast but a glance at riches, and they are gone, for they will surely
sprout wings and fly off to the sky like an eagle.

—PROVERBS 23:4–5

You guide me with your counsel,
and afterward you will take me into glory.

—PSALM 73:24

I can do everything through him who gives me strength.

—PHILIPPIANS 4:13

Your statutes are my delight; they are my counselors.

—PSALM 119:24

But those who hope in the LORD will renew their strength.
They will soar on wings like eagles; they will run and not grow weary,
they will walk and not be faint.

—ISAIAH 40:31

Praise be to the LORD God,
the God of Israel, who alone does marvelous deeds.

—Psalm 72:18

*Now faith is being sure of what we hope for
and certain of what we do not see.*

—HEBREWS 11:1

Those who sow in tears will reap with songs of joy.

—PSALM 126:5

*Do not be afraid. I bring you good news
of great joy that will be for all the people.*

—LUKE 2:10

From birth I have relied on you;
you brought me forth from my mother's womb.
I will ever praise you.

—PSALM 71:6

_____

_____

_____

_____

_____

_____

_____

_____

_____

_____

_____

_____

_____

_____

_____

_____

_____

_____

_____

_____

_____

_____

_Do_ not be anxious about anything, but in everything,
by prayer and petition, with thanksgiving, present your requests to God.
And the peace of God, which transcends all understanding,
will guard your hearts and your minds in Christ Jesus.

—PHILIPPIANS 4:6–7

You are a shield around me, O LORD;
you bestow glory on me and lift up my head.

—PSALM 3:3

And live a life of love, just as Christ loved us
and gave himself up for us as a fragrant offering and sacrifice to God.

—EPHESIANS 5:2

But from everlasting to everlasting
the LORD's love is with those who fear him,
and his righteousness with their children's children.

—PSALM 103:17–18

Yet I am not alone, for my Father is with me.

—JOHN 16:32

Know that the LORD is God.
It is he who made us, and we are his;
we are his people, the sheep of his pasture.

—PSALM 100:3

For you did not receive a spirit that makes you a slave again to fear, but you received the Spirit of sonship. . . . The Spirit himself testifies with our spirit that we are God's children.

—ROMANS 8:15–16

But I have stilled and quieted my soul;
like a weaned child with its mother,
like a weaned child is my soul within me.

—PSALM 131:2

_____

_____

_____

_____

_____

_____

_____

_____

_____

_____

_____

_____

_____

_____

_____

_____

_____

_____

_____

_____

_____

_____

Before they call I will answer;
while they are still speaking I will hear.

—ISAIAH 65:24

Delight yourself in the LORD
and he will give you the desires of your heart.

—PSALM 37:4

_____

_____

_____

_____

_____

_____

_____

_____

_____

_____

_____

_____

_____

_____

_____

_____

_____

_____

_____

_____

_____

_____